WHAT IS
REPENTANCE?

JEREMY WALKER

REFORMATION HERITAGE BOOKS
GRAND RAPIDS, MICHIGAN

What Is Repentance?
© 2015 by Jeremy Walker

All rights reserved. No part of this book may be used or reproduced in any manner whatsoever without written permission except in the case of brief quotations embodied in critical articles and reviews. Direct your requests to the publisher at the following addresses:

Reformation Heritage Books
3070 29th St. SE
Grand Rapids, MI 49512
616-977-0889
orders@heritagebooks.org
www.heritagebooks.org

Printed in the United States of America
22 23 24 25 26 27/10 9 8 7 6 5 4 3 2

ISBN 978-1-60178-431-5

For additional Reformed literature, request a free book list from Reformation Heritage Books at the above regular or e-mail address.

WHAT IS
REPENTANCE?

I have been privileged to visit a country where Christians were nicknamed "repenters." Is that a label that would suggest itself, let alone stick, in the society where you or I live? Would it readily apply to you? For many, *repentance* might be almost a dirty word, if it is used at all. I know one man, having been a Christian for about thirty years, who said that he had spent nearly twenty-five of those years in churches where repentance was never preached. To call for and to cultivate a spirit of repentance flies in the face of the spirit of our age; anything that threatens to make us feel bad about ourselves is frowned upon. Repentance is considered to be a terrible assault on our self-esteem, a tragic wounding of our sense of our own worth. Yet you cannot become a Christian without repentance. Similarly, you cannot remain a healthy child of God without repentance.

So what is *repentance*? It is, fundamentally, a thorough and radical change of the heart that results in a thorough and radical change of the life. We find one of the finest brief definitions in the Westminster Shorter Catechism and in some of its sister and daughter documents:

> Repentance unto life is a saving grace, whereby a sinner, out of a true sense of his sin, and apprehension of the mercy of God in Christ, does, with grief and hatred of his sin, turn from it unto God, with full purpose of, and endeavour after, new obedience.[1]

This definition captures briefly but superbly the biblical essence of repentance. I hope that as we work through this matter, this sweet summary will begin to glow with scriptural light and stir and encourage your soul.

We should begin by making plain that repentance belongs with faith. We cannot disentangle or divide these two graces, and no one should attempt to do so. As John Murray explains, "Saving faith is permeated with repentance and repentance is permeated with faith."[2] Christ saves through faith, and we should not give that place to repentance. Nevertheless, a faith that knows nothing of sorrow for sin with a yearning for holiness and increasingly complete obedience to the will of God in Christ is not a saving faith. As we will see, in the same way that we

---

1. In the Westminster Shorter Catechism, this is the answer to question 87. The language here is slightly updated.

2. John Murray, *Redemption Accomplished and Applied* (Edinburgh: Banner of Truth, 2009), 108.

need a repenting faith, so we need a believing repentance. Repentance is too often overlooked as faith's ugly cousin, when she ought to be celebrated as her beautiful twin sister.

In addressing the issue of repentance, it is helpful to have in mind a passage like 2 Corinthians 7:9–11:

> Now I rejoice, not that ye were made sorry, but that ye sorrowed to repentance: for ye were made sorry after a godly manner, that ye might receive damage by us in nothing. For godly sorrow worketh repentance to salvation not to be repented of: but the sorrow of the world worketh death. For behold this selfsame thing, that ye sorrowed after a godly sort, what carefulness it wrought in you, yea, what clearing of yourselves, yea, what indignation, yea, what fear, yea, what vehement desire, yea, what zeal, yea, what revenge! In all things ye have approved yourselves to be clear in this matter.

These words contain many of the elements that we must consider, and we will address some of them in specific detail. From this and other portions of our Bibles, we must identify some principles of repentance, glance at some portraits of repentance, and conclude with some thoughts on the practice of repentance.

PRINCIPLES OF REPENTANCE

Repentance lies at the heart of the gospel message. When the Lord Jesus sent out His disciples to proclaim the good news, He said, "Thus it is written, and thus it behooved Christ to suffer, and to rise from the dead the third day: and that repentance and remission of sins should be preached in his name among all nations, beginning at Jerusalem" (Luke 24:46–47). Sinners are at least as much drawn to repentance by divine goodness as they are driven by personal guilt: "Despisest thou the riches of his goodness and forbearance and longsuffering; not knowing that the goodness of God leadeth thee to repentance?" (Rom. 2:4). Repentance belongs pre-eminently to the gospel by way of gift, command, promise, motive, and purpose. It is a matter of grace and a fruit of mercy. Without a believing grasp of God's mercy, "there may be a sense of sin as hurtful to the sinner himself, but not a sense of it as hateful to a holy God."[3] At the same time, a sinner without a sense of God as merciful in Christ will fly from Him and not to Him. Sinclair Ferguson writes:

> Only when we turn away from looking at our own sin to look at the face of God, to find his pardoning grace, do we begin to repent. Only by seeing that there is grace and forgiveness with him would we ever dare to repent and thus return to the fellowship and presence of the Father.[4]

---

3. John Colquhoun, *Repentance* (Edinburgh: Banner of Truth, 2010), 13.

4. Sinclair Ferguson, *The Christian Life: A Doctrinal Introduction* (Edinburgh: Banner of Truth, 2013), 69.

The Lord told the parable of the prodigal son to underline God's eagerness to receive the repenting sinner: there is joy in heaven over one sinner who repents!

Gospel repentance is the Spirit-wrought, heart-felt response to God's pardoning mercy offered in Christ, a response made by a sinner convinced of his sin. Christ said, "I came not to call the righteous, but sinners to repentance" (Luke 5:32). When the sinner hears that call effectually, he is convicted by the Holy Spirit of sin, of righteousness, and of judgment (John 16:8–11). So convicted, and discerning that God in Christ is ready to bestow forgiveness upon those who repent and believe, he turns from his sin to God. In so turning, he desires to be forever free of that which offends the Holy One and to be marked increasingly by the righteousness that is pleasing to Him.

We see something of these negative and positive aspects of repentance in the pressing call of the prophet Isaiah: "Let the wicked forsake his way, and the unrighteous man his thoughts: and let him return unto the LORD, and he will have mercy upon him; and to our God, for he will abundantly pardon" (Isa. 55:7). The whole context is scented with Christ, for the promised Servant and atoning Savior has just been set forth.

Turning from Sin

Repentance is not a passing expression of regret or sorrow that focuses on the trouble that comes with sin rather than on the sin itself. The true repenter never wants to have his cake and to eat it, to enjoy peace with God while still indulging in sin. Rather, the wicked man recognizes his wickedness and the guilt it brings in the eyes of a holy God and turns his back upon the entire pattern of his godless life. He does not seek or offer a little reformation here and there, a tidying up of the rough edges. He does not sin in the hope that he can use repentance as an excuse to go on sinning. Rather, he rejects and renounces his sinful habits. The unrighteous man, who now sees that he provokes God to anger by his lack of goodness, leaves behind all the designs and purposes that run contrary to the holy will.

We should notice several things about this turning from sin. First, it is something that *sinners* do. God's gospel is not addressed to those who have sorted themselves out, tidied up their messy lives, got their spiritual act together, and manufactured some kind of acceptability before God. Mercy is offered to the lost and miserable. There are no preconditions.

Second, although we often like to divide up sins into categories or degrees, the repentance dealt with here is repentance for all and any sins. While it is true that there are some particularly vile, scandalous, distasteful, or great sins (1 Cor. 5:1) and that some people can be accounted great sinners (see 1 Tim. 1:15), no sin in itself is small (Rom. 3:23). Each requires to be covered with the blood of Jesus Christ. Every sin is grievous, an offense against God's holy law, and to stumble in one point is to be guilty of all (James 2:10). The repentance required of sinners is for every known sin. Every sin is fundamentally against God, an expression of a heart in rebellion.

That is why when David contemplates his adultery and murder he cries out, "Against thee, thee only, have I sinned, and done this evil in thy sight: that thou mightest be justified when thou speakest, and be clear when thou judgest" (Ps. 51:4). Is David suggesting that sin has no impact on the horizontal plane? That it has no effect on other people? Is David ignoring his sin against Uriah, whose wife he stole and whose death he orchestrated; or Bathsheba, whom—perhaps with some measure of complicity from her—he took to his bed? What about the others caught up in and affected directly or indirectly by his transgressions?

Of course sin is against other creatures! When a husband snaps angrily at his wife, she is not an irrelevance in the matter of sin. When a child snarls at his parents, there is an offense there to address.

But this is not the primary dimension. Sin is defined first and foremost as that which is against God. That is the direction in which it forms and the line along which its foulness and filthiness fully develop. The apostle John tells us that "whosoever committeth sin transgresseth also the law: for sin is the transgression of the law" (1 John 3:4). Biblically defined, sin assumes a standard—a perfect law that is written and established in the conscience. Sin presumes a deviation in principle and practice against or away from that law. Sin also requires an accounting because there is a Lawgiver to whom we must answer for our transgressions. Sin demands a punishment—God's righteous judgment either in us or in an appointed representative. So sin needs an answer, and the only full and final answer it ever finds is Jesus Christ, with the forgiveness of and freedom from sins offered in Him who was manifested to take away our sins and in whom there is no sin (1 John 3:5).

You will never understand what older writers called "the sinfulness of sin" until you see sin as that which is against God. His infinite holiness and divine majesty are the only context in which sin is truly seen and understood. This is why every sin is damnable: because it must be measured not only by what it is in itself, but also by the One against whom it is committed. Being committed against the infinite holiness of the Holy One, a rebellion against the all-encompassing righteousness of the righteous Lord, sin is an offense of infinite magnitude. A single sin not dealt with is sufficient to take us to hell.

Third, and taking all this into account, repentance must be for particular sins. It is too easy to denounce sin as an abstract thing rather than repent of concrete sins that occur in real situations and really offend the real God as well as really damage other real relationships. General declarations of repentance ("For any sins that we might have committed...") and vague and impersonal expressions of confession ("If we have in any way offended Thee…") are often merely a way of sloping the shoulders, deflecting the point, defending the reputation, and denying the reality of the sin.

When we come under conviction of sin and begin to repent, we start at last to name and shame our sins. We see the holy lines that God has drawn and how we have trampled over and across them. The person with a perpetually angry spirit no longer blames the failures of others for provoking him or her to frustration, but considers the root of pride in the heart. The man or woman who has been getting sexual thrills by gazing at pornography starts honestly to face his or her selfish and adulterous heart. The teenager fantasizing about a sexual relationship with a teacher mourns over his appetite for fornication. The young woman who has dressed suggestively and flirted eagerly considers her desperation to be the center of attention. The woman who assaults and undermines the reputations of others with a vicious stream of gossip feels its wickedness. The man who bullies and shoves verbally and physically grieves over his desire to sit enthroned over every creature. The children who have been happy lying so long as Dad or Mom do not find out can no longer excuse themselves. The mother who has resented her responsibilities to her husband and children faces the fact. The husband who, as a spiritual head, has lazily neglected to nurture his family stops making excuses. The largely prayerless Christian is appalled by the pride revealed through living as if there is no need of God's grace. The arrogant and pushy church member is sickened by the way in which he or she has trampled on the consciences of the saints and kicked against the authority of Christ's appointed undershepherds. All of this is, and is known and felt to be, contrary to the will and word of almighty God. When we begin to see sin as God sees sin, then we begin to identify it and grieve over it accordingly.

In each such instance, the honest man—dealing faithfully with his own soul and with his God—makes specific confession. David McIntyre puts it this way:

> Confession of sin should be explicit.... Standing beside the ruins of Jericho, Joshua said to Achan, "My son, give, I pray thee, glory to the Lord God of Israel, and make confession unto Him." And Achan answered, "Indeed, I have sinned against the Lord God of Israel; *and thus and thus have I done*" (Josh. 7:19, 20, emphasis added).
>
> The great promise of the New Testament is not less definite: "If we confess our sins, He is faithful and just to forgive us our sins, and to cleanse us from all unrighteousness" (1 John 1:9).
>
> A wise old writer says, "A child of God will confess sin in particular; an unsound Christian will confess sin by wholesale; he will acknowledge he is a sinner in general; whereas David doth, as it were, point with his finger to the sore: 'I have done this evil' (Psa. 51:4); he doth not say,

'I have done evil,' but 'this evil.' He points to his blood-guiltiness."[5]

Fourth, we must recognize the difference between mere remorse and true repentance. We must not confuse the presence of tears with genuine repentance—they do not necessarily belong together. (Indeed, some people even weep because they cannot sin, at least not with the freedom that they might wish. Their opportunity to indulge in wickedness has been taken away! This is certainly not repentance.) Remorse may be an expression of sorrow over wrongdoing, but it often focuses only on the guilt or consequences of sin. Remorse is more like despair over sin. It has no sense of God's mercy; it never runs to Him. We see it in the history of biblical characters like Ahab and Judas. As we have already seen, repentance is not fear of or despair over the consequences of sin, nor is it a carnal resolve to stop sinning. It is not a temporary departure from sin or a slight distancing of ourselves from sin. You can hate the effects and consequences of sin without ever hating sin itself. You can be sorry that you were caught stealing, or you can hate the fact that you stole. False repentance fears the judgment of the law but does not honor the justice of the law. True repentance is the realization that you have sinned against God, and not just the

---

5. David McIntyre, *The Hidden Life of Prayer* (Fearn, Ross-shire, Scotland: Christian Focus, 2010), 80.

fear of being caught or the regret that—having been caught—you must now be punished. Repentance is not a mere change of feeling, but a change of heart and mind, permanent rather than transient, thorough rather than shallow.

And this brings us to the root of the matter. "Repentance is a thorough change of man's natural heart upon the subject of sin."[6] You begin to see sin in your heart from what is essentially the divine perspective, and that creates a thoroughgoing horror and hatred of sin in the soul. Repentance involves accurate knowledge of sin, true sorrow for sin, real confession of sin, sincere shame over sin, deep hatred of sin, and a thorough departure from sin. D. Martyn Lloyd-Jones explains,

> Repentance means that you realize that you are a guilty, vile sinner in the presence of God, that you deserve the wrath and punishment of God, that you are hell-bound. It means that you begin to realize that this thing called sin is in you, that you long to get rid of it, and that you turn your back on it in every shape and form. You renounce the world whatever the cost, the world in its mind and outlook as well as its practice, and you deny yourself, and take up the cross and go after Christ.[7]

6. J. C. Ryle, *Old Paths* (Edinburgh: Banner of Truth, 1999), 405.

7. D. Martyn Lloyd-Jones, *Studies in the Sermon on the Mount* (London: Inter-Varsity Fellowship, 1960), 2:248.

Repentance, then, is a turning from sin. To quote Ryle once more, "To say that we are sorry for our sins is mere hypocrisy, unless we show that we are really sorry for them, by giving them up. Doing is the very life of repentance."[8] But it is also something more than a turning from sin. The eighteenth-century Scottish preacher John Colquhoun said, "This godly sorrow for sin and this holy abhorrence of it arise from a spiritual discovery of pardoning mercy with God in Christ, and from the exercise of trusting in his mercy."[9] As we have already identified, alongside the turning from sin there is also a turning to God.

Turning to God

In Isaiah 55:7 the repenter turns from sin to God, eager to know, love, and serve Him. He comes thirsty to the fountain of living waters; he comes starving to the bread of life; he comes poor to the great Giver; he comes disappointed to the abundance of God; he comes empty to the fullness of Him who fills all in all. John Murray reminds us of the essential character of repentance, but also presses home that it affects more than our opinion of sin: "Repentance consists essentially in change of heart and mind and will. The change of heart and mind and will principally respects four things: it is a change of mind

---

8. J. C. Ryle, *Expository Thoughts on the Gospels: Luke* (Edinburgh: Banner of Truth, 2012), 1:80.

9. Colquhoun, *Repentance*, 3.

respecting God, respecting ourselves, respecting sin, and respecting righteousness."[10]

So here is the sinner turning back to the very One against whom he has been rebelling. He seeks the face of the One whom he has been offending. Out of darkness, he desires light. Out of death, he longs for the life that comes from knowing God Almighty (John 17:3). In its context, this invitation to return to the Lord is astounding in its breadth, for it goes out not just to Jews but to the nations of the earth (see Isa. 55:5), assuring all that those who seek the Lord will find Him. He will turn away none who come to Him (see John 6:37). Perhaps such a sinner might come to God with something of Job's spirit: "Though he slay me, yet will I trust in him" (Job 13:15). He comes trembling, conscious of his genuine deserving of death and his profound unworthiness to receive a blessing, and yet he cannot *not* come! The sinner comes with all his sin's guilt clinging to him but loathed by him. But however the sinner feels about himself and his sin, he also knows that he must have God. This sense of heartfelt grief over and loathing for sin with the same desire for a merciful God is urged by Joel: "Rend your heart, and not your garments, and turn unto the LORD your God: for he is gracious and merciful, slow to anger, and of great kindness, and repenteth him of the evil" (Joel 2:13).

---

10. Murray, *Redemption Accomplished and Applied*, 108.

It is precisely the same pattern that the apostle Paul describes when he speaks of the experience of the Thessalonians as the gospel came to them not in word only, but in power and in the Holy Spirit and in much assurance: "For they themselves shew of us what manner of entering in we had unto you, and how ye turned to God from idols to serve the living and true God; and to wait for his Son from heaven, whom he raised from the dead, even Jesus, which delivered us from the wrath to come" (1 Thess. 1:9–10). All God's people in every age have been repenters.

Again, we must make certain things plain. First, real repentance always involves this turning from and turning to. Repentance issues in the pursuit of God and godliness, usually along precisely the same line as the sin repented of and in the diametrically opposed direction, whether or not that is seen in the broadest strokes or in the fine details of life. There is the same breadth and particularity here, and the same dependence upon God in Christ. So the idolater will cast away his idols and be a worshiper of God alone. The angry man will repent of his anger and will pursue—not perfectly but persistently and increasingly—self-control over his own spirit. The man who curses will turn his back upon cutting and coarse speech and cultivate instead the wholesome tongue, which is a tree of life (Prov. 15:4). The pornographer will seek to cut off every channel through which filthy words and images flow into his life and patiently wait for or seek sexual satisfaction only through the legitimate means appointed by God. The gossip will seek to speak words of life and health rather than wounding cruelty. The proud bully will humble himself before God and men and walk in meekness. The lying child will seek always to speak truth. The resentful or careless wife and mother will cultivate a sacrificial spirit and invest in the sphere in which the Lord has graciously placed her. The lazy father will prayerfully establish patterns of righteous spiritual headship in his family, denying his sluggish inclinations. We will find the careless saint on his or her knees, clinging to Christ the rock and pleading with God for present forgiveness and daily grace. Arrogant church members will begin to esteem others better than themselves and cultivate a more properly Berean spirit toward their pastors and teachers.

Second, repentance is not virtuous in and of itself. Repentance does not merit God's favor or oblige Him to pardon; it is not the effective cause of God pardoning our sins. Satisfaction for our sin is the work of Christ alone. To rely upon our repentance as in any way entitling us to or meriting God's favor would be to take the glory from Christ and to make our salvation depend upon a good work. In one sense, even our repentance is sinful—we might repent of our repentance, for not one of us truly realizes the gravity and awfulness of his sin! We must never confuse the scriptural idea of penitence with the notion of doing penance. To do penance implies that there are works that we can do to counterbalance our sinfulness and sins. But true repentance is not a system of weights and balances whereby we can somehow atone, by ourselves and in our own right, for an equal and opposite weight of sin. Our repentance is *not* the ground upon which we rest for the satisfaction of divine justice, and penance is not a virtue by means of which man merits God's favor. Salvation is not of works—not even of works that are good in themselves—lest any man should have grounds for boasting (Eph. 2:8–9). Such an attitude would make repentance an enemy of faith rather than her twin grace.

Here, then, are these conjoined elements in repentance: "Let the wicked forsake his way, and the unrighteous man his thoughts: and let him return unto the LORD, and he will have mercy upon him; and to our God, for he will abundantly pardon" (Isa. 55:7). This, and this only, is repentance: turning from sin with hatred of it and turning to God with eagerness for Him. Without repentance there can be no escape from hell or peace with God. Unless we repent, we shall all perish (Luke 13:5).

But do you see the promise that is then bound up in God's declaration? Whoever abandons sin and seeks God will discover, in returning to the Lord, all the depths of divine goodness in which he had trusted. God will have mercy! God will abundantly pardon! This is no mere possibility but an absolute assurance. Subjectively, the repenting sinner discovers all the surging love of the divine heart, all the wonder of the Almighty's undeserved favor as the Lord welcomes that sinner, and he finds all his expectation as much exceeded as the prodigal son upon his return to his father (Luke 15:21–22). Objectively, the repenting sinner finds divine mercy exercised in the abundant pardon of all his sins, for the atonement of the Lamb of God secures the righteous putting away of sin, the pardon of all kinds of sin committed by all kinds of sinners.

True repentance invariably meets a favorable response from a gracious God: How could it not when it is both His grand desire (2 Peter 3:9) and His gracious gift (Acts 11:18; 2 Tim. 2:25)? God offers Himself on the most gracious and glorious terms: "Repent ye therefore, and be converted, that your sins may be blotted out, when the times of refreshing shall come from the presence of the Lord" (Acts 3:19). We can come to God as we are, but we cannot stay as we are. Those despairing of their own strength cry out to God, "Turn thou me, and I shall be turned; for thou art the LORD my God" (Jer. 31:18).

We must also be clear that these principles worked out in the soul are always manifest: the forsaking of the sinful way and the unrighteous thoughts with the turning to a merciful and pardoning God invariably produce appropriate fruit (Matt. 3:8). Where there is inward humiliation there is always outward reformation. A change of heart must result in a change of life.

When Paul preached in obedience to the heavenly vision he had received, he "shewed first unto them of Damascus, and at Jerusalem, and throughout all the coasts of Judaea, and then to the Gentiles, that they should repent and turn to God, and do works meet for repentance" (Acts 26:19–20). The same apostle said to the Corinthians that

> godly sorrow worketh repentance to salvation not to be repented of: but the sorrow of the world worketh death. For behold this selfsame thing, that ye sorrowed after a godly sort, what carefulness it wrought in you, yea, what clearing of yourselves, yea, what indignation, yea, what fear, yea, what vehement desire, yea, what zeal, yea, what revenge! In all things ye have approved yourselves to be clear in this matter. (2 Cor. 7:10–11)

As a tree is known by its fruit, so is repentance.

The repenting sinner is diligent and earnest, profoundly aware of the seriousness of the situation and the sinfulness of sin, and therefore careful to avoid all temptations to and occasions of sin. He clears himself, repenting of his own sin, rectifying known faults, and refusing to indulge the sinful principles and practices of the world around him. He is indignant, offended by sin in all its forms and expressions, especially as he finds it breaking out in his own heart. He is fearful, trembling because of the hatefulness of sin to the God he loves and the painfulness of sin to his own soul, fleeing his own unwilling inclinations toward that which he loathes. He is full of vehement desires that the power of sin should be broken in him for the uprooting of vice and the cultivation of virtue, addressing the effects of sin in relationships both with God and man. He is zealous now for the glory of God, for purity in his own life and in the church of Christ, for obedience to the teaching of righteousness. He vindicates himself, showing his new status and declaring his righteous appetites, and aims by a thoroughgoing campaign against sin throughout his redeemed humanity, taking vengeance on wickedness wherever it is or has been expressed, and so making full reparation and restoration wherever and whenever he is able. So the repenter proves himself clear in this matter.

No one is saved unless he repents. True repentance is necessary before God will pardon our sins, because such sorrow for sin and turning from sin is the response of a regenerate heart. When God in sovereign mercy creates the heart of man anew, the Spirit of God invariably works both faith and repentance in the heart of that man and moves them to the fruitful pursuit of new obedience. We are saved through faith in Christ's glorious person and finished work and not because of repentance as the effective cause of our salvation. However, we are not saved without faith in Christ and repentance unto life. Again, this is not to make repentance a precondition of mercy, but to put it in its proper place. Lloyd-Jones says, "No man can experience the Christian salvation unless he knows what it is to repent."[11] The eighteenth-century Baptist pastor and scholar John Fawcett emphasized the proper relationship between faith and repentance when he said,

> True faith is connected with repentance of sin. If we are not turned from sin to God, if sin is not made bitter to us, if it does not appear hateful, if our hearts are not penetrated with sorrow, grief, and self-abhorrence on account of it, in vain do we imagine ourselves to be believers in Jesus. Looking unto him whom we have pierced, is accompanied with mourning and bitterness of soul. That faith which leaves the heart impenitent is not saving; for repentance is absolutely necessary for salvation. Our blessed Redeemer said to a certain woman in the gospel, "Thy faith hath saved thee, go in peace." But what was the attendant of the faith she possessed? Was it not penitence?… Repentance is justly said by some, to be the tear of love dropping from the eye of faith.[12]

PORTRAITS OF REPENTANCE

When we look at the biblical record, we find the principles sketched out above borne out in practice. In briefly looking at various scriptural portraits of repentance, we must be careful not to standardize the

---

11. D. Martyn Lloyd-Jones, *Out of the Depths* (Bryntirion: Evangelical Press of Wales, 1991), 12.

12. John Fawcett, *Christ Precious* (Minneapolis, Minn.: Klock & Klock, 1979), 22–23.

outward expressions of true penitence. We must not make prescriptive what is only descriptive. We might pray for the gift of repenting tears, but they are for God to store in a bottle and to record in His book (Ps. 56:8), not for us to count as if a certain number must be shed before we have really repented.

The realities and the results of repentance are more or less plain in every genuine instance of this grace. They are lacking in Cain's terrors, Pharaoh's assurances, Ahab's humiliations, Herod's performances, and Judas's confessions. They are present, in some form or other, in the positive models the Lord gives us of repenting hearts.

Something of all this is found in the parable that includes the story of the prodigal son (Luke 15:11–31). While God's readiness to receive the repenter is central and the matter of repentance is more incidental, there are still instructive elements. The son, having turned his back upon his father, eventually comes to himself. There is a radical reassessment of the way he has been thinking, speaking, and acting with regard to his father and about himself and his behavior. There is a desire to return humbly, begging for forgiveness as one who deserves nothing. There is a sincere following through on that intention. And there is the magnificent and munificent response of the father, gathering the erring, repenting, returning son into his arms and lavishing upon him all the marks of unfettered affection and delight. Can we imagine that the restored son does not now live a life of cheerful, willing, grateful, and obedient service from that point on, seeking to be everything that a true son should be?

Similar features are there in the tax collector in the temple (Luke 18:13). As the Pharisee prays his boomerang prayer, which settles back upon himself in all his imagined virtue, the tax collector prays his bullet prayer. Here is a "sinner's prayer" indeed! He assumes the right position, describing himself as "a sinner,"[13] conscious of his great wickedness in the eyes of God, making a personal and individual confession of his own wretchedness and hopelessness. He approaches the right person: God here is no audience to a performance but the offended Judge of all the earth—and his Judge. He has business with the Holy One, and so he beats his breast and cannot lift his eyes to heaven. And yet he adopts the right petition, for he knows that only one thing can bridge the gap between the offended God and the offending sinner: "God be merciful to me a sinner!" In the place where blood was shed for the remission of sins, he asks that God would be propitiated with regard to him, that He would turn away His divine wrath and put away the sinner's sin because of a substitutionary sacrifice. And this is the man who goes back to his house that day declared to be righteous in the sight of a propitiated and pardoning God.

---

13. Literally, "the sinner." It is as if he alone must face the Lord his God.

The features are there, too, in the conversion of Zacchaeus (Luke 19:1–10). At first only curious, he responds to the condescension of Christ, who calls the little man to Himself. Repentance is a response to a divine initiative, one of the initial acts of a heart stirred by the call of God to a sinner. Then, Zacchaeus makes a particular and personal response to his particular and personal sins. He not only acknowledges the truth of the general charge laid against him publicly that he is a sinner, but he goes further: "Behold, Lord, the half of my goods I give to the poor; and if I have taken any thing from any man by false accusation, I restore him fourfold" (Luke 19:8). His penitence is not vague or evasive. He accuses himself with unerring accuracy and unrelenting severity. He deals with himself as he knows himself to be. Furthermore, all this happens "this day" (Luke 19:9). Zacchaeus does not defer his response to a later date, but immediately sets in motion the wheels of repentant righteousness. There is no misty promise that "I *will* give," but rather a definite action: "Behold… I give." Delays so often prove fatal in this matter. It is too easy to resolve something while hearing a sermon or reading a book, and yet by the time we come to act upon it, we have talked ourselves out of a righteous spiritual impulse in response to conviction of sin. Not so Zacchaeus! His repentance was deep and costly. The radical reversal of his priorities and pursuits bit into his bank balance in a big way. The idol is toppled! Nothing is spared! The weeds of sin are utterly uprooted! Zacchaeus accounts himself a thief, and his righteousness in repentance exceeds that of the Pharisees, going beyond what the law might strictly have required. Though radical and painful, Zacchaeus carries out this repentance voluntarily and completely, not grudgingly. Zacchaeus is not coached through it, nor is his arm twisted. He has no regrets that this cancer of sin is being cut out of his life. He does not return to his sin like a dog to its vomit (2 Peter 2:22), but expresses the new direction of his renewed heart in godly fear. And note, too, how this is a positive and active demonstration. The taker has become a giver. The thief has become a benefactor. The greedy hoarder has become a generous distributor. The cunning deceiver is now a man of scrupulous honesty. Sin gives way to and is displaced by grace at the very point of conflict.

Do you see how repentance invariably manifests itself in real, substantial changes to the attitudes, affections, and actions of a person? Where there is a change of heart there is always a change of life. The Bible both tells us and shows us the nature and effects of true repentance.

PRACTICING REPENTANCE

You may know that some of the streams that fed into the Reformation mingled together on the day a monk named Martin Luther, in the city of Wittenberg, nailed theological propositions to the door of the Castle Church, opening up certain questions for discussion and debate. The first of those Ninety-Five Theses was this: "When our Lord and Master, Jesus Christ, said 'Repent,' He called for the entire life of believers to be one of repentance."

Repentance toward God—like faith in Christ—is to be continually characteristic of all true Christians. They are not just the double doors through which a believer enters the way of life; they are the shoes he wears to walk the whole way. True Christians, through many battles and trials, never stop believing in the Lord Jesus, and we never stop turning away from sin and to God as we discover it in our hearts:

> If we say that we have fellowship with him, and walk in darkness, we lie, and do not the truth: but if we walk in the light, as he is in the light, we have fellowship one with another, and the blood of Jesus Christ his Son cleanseth us from all sin. If we say that we have no sin, we deceive ourselves, and the truth is not in us. If we confess our sins, he is faithful and just to forgive us our sins, and to cleanse us from all unrighteousness. If we say that we have not sinned, we make him a liar, and his word is not in us. (1 John 1:6–10)

The cleansing that we enjoy, through God's pardoning mercy in Christ Jesus, is not just an initial act but an ongoing blessing with regard to those continued sins over which we go on repenting. We must live close to the fountain opened for sin and for uncleanness (Zech. 13:1) and go there often as the passage of time uncovers more and more of the sins of commission and omission in our hearts and lives. It would do us well to remember that David's penitent cries in Psalm 51 are the confessions and concerns of a backslider, not an unbeliever. This is the man after God's own heart who sinned against his God and his Lord. Repentance is not a plant that flourishes only along the first yards of our journey to heaven, only to wither and die before we have traveled very far. Rather, it is a grace that—rooted in our fellowship with Christ Jesus—grows steadily and bears fruit increasingly all through our lives.

Have you ever come to yourself and realized that you need to return to God? Have you ever prayed with a heart like the tax collector in the temple, "God be merciful to me a sinner!"? Have you made a particular and personal repentance for your particular and personal sins, however deep and costly, and have you done it willingly and cheerfully, positively and actively? These are some of the sure evidences of conversion. If you do not have them, consider sin's horrors and God's mercies, and you will soon be fleeing to the cross. Cry to God for a tender heart, search your soul in the light of God's Word, pray for the gift of repenting tears, and turn to God from your idols.

And do you labor to maintain a Word-instructed and Spirit-worked sensitivity to sin in thought, word, and deed? Healthy Christians are perpetually tenderhearted with regard to sin. Indeed, it would not be unusual for Christians to feel more convinced of their sins the closer their relationship to Christ. The more they walk in the light, the more clearly they see the horror of their transgressions as well as the pardoning mercy of their God and the saving sufficiency of their Redeemer. Repentance is not a stage you pass through on the way to heaven, but the path you travel all the way, as John Murray observes: "The broken spirit and the contrite heart are abiding marks of the believing soul."[14] Never cease in the battle against sin, and never cease to call upon the Lord for mercy for sins committed as the battle rages. Cultivate that holy fear of God that is conscious of living in His presence and hates to offend Him: "If thou, LORD, shouldest mark iniquities, O Lord, who shall stand? But there is forgiveness with thee, that thou mayest be feared" (Ps. 130:3–4).

Further, do you continue to bring forth fruits worthy of repentance? Remember that a change of heart invariably leads to a change of life. Has your godly sorrow over sin produced repentance leading to salvation, not to be regretted? Does it continue to produce a diligent care that avoids sin? Does it produce a clearing of yourself, so that you still repent of and resist sins? Are you indignant toward sin, counting it a hateful offense toward God and the enemy that Christ died to overcome in you? Do you fear sin as obnoxious to the God whom you love? Do you eagerly long to see sin shattered in your experience?

---

14. Murray, *Redemption Accomplished and Applied*, 110.

Are you zealous for good works and God's glory? Do your thoughts, speech, and behavior vindicate your profession to be a follower of Christ Jesus? Are you proving yourself clear in this matter? Does a costly but willing, painful but cheerful, deep but eager repentance continue to be clear in your life as you root out all known sin and put it to death through the grace and power of the risen Christ?

Repentance was a keynote of our Lord's ministry alongside of the call to come to Him to be saved. There is no pardon without repentance, no lasting joy without this godly sorrow. Unless we repent, we will all perish (Luke 13:5). If we repent, though our sins are scarlet, the Lord will make them as white as snow.

No one can ever be truly happy who has not learned to grieve over sin. There is no joy like the joy of sins forgiven, and those who would journey to heaven must do so on a stream of repenting tears and with the wind of faith in their sails. Are you a repenter? In this matter all of us must ask ourselves the same question that once impressed itself on the soul of John Bunyan: "Will you leave your sins and go to heaven, or have your sins and go to hell?"[15]

Remember that the Lord is gracious and merciful, slow to anger and of great kindness, quick to forgive. So let us forsake every wicked way and every

---

15. John Bunyan, *Grace Abounding to the Chief of Sinners*, in *Works of John Bunyan*, ed. George Offor (Edinburgh: Banner of Truth, 1991), 1:8 (§22), language updated.

unrighteous thought. Let us—with all our hearts, even with fasting and mourning—rend our hearts and return to the Lord, who will have mercy upon us. Turn to the Lord your God, for He will abundantly pardon.